This book belongs to

____

Impressum:

Kevin Götz
Lister Kirchweg 57
D-30163

Kevin.goetz@hotmail.de

Made in the USA
Las Vegas, NV
24 February 2021

18201320R10066